BLOOMING
IN
motion

COLORING BOOK BY
AMBER BARBEE PICKENS

Published in the United States by Art Belongs to People Publishing Company. For information, address Art Belongs to People Publishing Company, P.O. Box 222139, Dallas, TX 75222. www.bloominginmotion.com

This book may be purchased in bulk for promotional, educational, or business use. Please contact The Marketing Collaborative at (212) 920-9147, or email info@bloominginmotion.com.

Original Illustrations by Amber Barbee Pickens

Cover artwork by Amber Barbee Pickens

Cover and book design by Heather R. Sanders, A Sanders Company®

Interior book layout by Cory Broussard, Artistic Embodiment LLC.

ISBN: 978-1-7362380-0-4

Printed in the United States

Distributed by Ingram Book Company

First Edition: December 2020

1 2 3 4 5 20 21 22 23 24 25

BLOOMING

IN

motion

To the trailblazers,

    For your tremendous fearlessness, perseverance,
sacrifice, discipline, and eternal resilience.

May the essence of your souls continue to live on stage

Love,
    Amber

amber's coloring tips

Coloring has filled my artistic tank in many ways that I hope for you as well. I encourage markers, crayons, colored pencils, gel pens, and whatever else awakens your inner artist. I love using colored pencils because they allow me to create fine lines, mix colors, and dimension by shading.

BE FREE.
BE INVINCIBLE.
BE MESSY.
BE GROUNDED.
BE FUELED.
BE EXPANSIVE.
BE LOUD.
BE MOVED.

EXPLORE.
CREATE.
INSPIRE.
TELL YOUR STORY.

Alvin Ailey (January 5, 1931-December 1, 1989)

Arthur Mitchell (March 27, 1934-September 19, 2018)

Asadata Dafora (August 4, 1890-March 4, 1965)

Bill "Bojangles" Robinson (May 25, 1878–November 25, 1949)

Carmen de Lavallade (March 6, 1931)

Debbie Allen (January 16, 1950)

Eartha Kitt (January 17, 1927–December 25, 2008)

Florence Mills (January 25, 1896–November 1,1927)

Frankie Manning (May 26, 1914–April 27,2009)

Geoffrey Holder (August 1, 1930–October 5, 2014)

Janet Collins (March 7, 1917–March 28, 2003)

John W. Bubbles (February 19, 1902–May 18, 1986)

Josephine Baker (June 3, 1906–April 12, 1975)

Katherine Dunham (June 22, 1909–May 21, 2006)

Nicholas Brothers: Fayard Nicholas (October 20, 1914–January 24, 2006)

Harold Nicholas (March 2, 1921-July 3, 2000)

Norma Miller (December 2, 1919–May 5, 2019)

Pearl Primus (November 29, 1919–October 29, 1994)

Raven Wilkinson (February 2, 1935–December 1, 2018)

Amber Barbee Pickens (January 28, 1993)

alvin ailey

"Dance is for everybody.
I believe that the dance came from
the people and that it should always
be delivered back to the people."

arthur mitchell

"What does dance give you?
The freedom to be who you are and do
what you want to do."

asadata dafora

"I would very much like to present patterns of African culture with a regard to artistic truth."

bill "bojangles" robinson

"What success I achieved in the theater is due to the fact that I have always worked just as hard when there were ten people in the house as when there were thousands."

carmen
de lavallade

"Dance is also universal. You can take it
any place and people will understand it,
because it's a language everyone speaks."

debbie allen

"Failure: Is it a limitation?

But out of limitations comes creativity."

eartha kitt

"You don't move just to because
you want to go from this point to that
point – the body has to be using the words
as well as you vocally use the words."

florence mills

"I don't care where I am
so long as I can sing and dance."

coloring

promotes creativity, meditation, and reduced anxiety. While focusing on the present, we're able to achieve mindfulness and increase positive thoughts. Coloring inspires my inner artist to embrace relaxation.

dancing

creates a safe space for expression and
abandonment of daily judgment.
For many, it serves as a time of sheer
freedom to let loose and have fun. When
I dance, I try to become one with the
music and go on an unknown journey.

frankie manning

"I've never seen a Lindy Hopper who wasn't smiling. It's a happy dance. It makes you feel good."

geoffrey
holder

"I always wanted to know what it felt like
to fall on stage...now I know.
It's not how you fall, but how you get up."

janet collins

"You don't get there because
you get there in spite of."

john w. bubbles

"Tap is just about the hardest thing to explain. Just keep on tapping along. That's about the size of it."

josephine baker

"I love performing.

I shall perform until the day I die."

katherine dunham

"Go within every day and find the inner strength so that the world will not blow your candle out."

"I copied my brother.
He was a natural dancer.
Graceful. People always
asked did we study ballet.
We never did."
–Harold Nicholas

nicholas brothers

"My brother and I used our whole bodies,
our hands, our personalities and everything.
We tried to make it classic.
We called our type of dancing classical tap
and we just hoped the audience liked it."
–Fayard Nicholas

norma miller

"I'm happy to say, Swing is here to stay."

pearl primus

"Why do I dance? Dance is my medicine.
It's the scream which eases for a while
the terrible frustration common to all
human beings who because of race,
creed, or color, are 'invisible'.
Dance is the fist with which I fight the
sickening ignorance of prejudice."

raven wilkinson

"Ballet is a very dedicated, hard road to hoe.
What kept me going was hope—hope for myself,
hope for everyone else and I have hope for this
beautiful artistic expression – not just ballet but dance.
It's a very special privilege to be a part of something
that speaks to people so meaningfully and
takes them out of their everyday lives."

amber barbee pickens

"I feel free when I dance...
it's an escape and a way of praise.
I dance as a testimony of God's grace –
it's my release."

dancer bios

1. **Alvin Ailey** (January 5, 1931–December 1, 1989) Alvin Ailey was a dancer, choreographer, activist, and founder of the Alvin Ailey American Dance Theater. Ailey choreographed close to 80 ballets over the span of his career. Ailey's iconic ballet, Revelations, was inspired by his 'blood memories' in rural Texas and the Baptist Church. His timeless choreography has been recognized around the world. Today, the Alvin American Dance Theater is the world's largest modern dance company.

2. **Arthur Mitchell** (March 27, 1934–September 19,2018)Arthur Mitchell was a dancer, choreographer, director, and founder of the Dance Theater of Harlem. He was the first African American to become a principal dancer with a major ballet company, New York City Ballet. After attending the High School for the Performing Arts in NYC, he began performing in many Broadway musicals and with companies of Donald McKayle and John Butler. After becoming a principal dancer at New York City Ballet, George Balanchine created several roles for him in ballets such as A Midsummer Night's Dream and Agon. He founded Dance Theater of Harlem out of determination to create an all-black dance company.

3. **Asadata Dafora** (August 4, 1890–March 4, 1965) Asadata Dafora was a dancer, choreographer, director, musician, and writer. He is credited for bringing authentic West African culture in theatrical form to American audiences in the 1930s. This led to a western appreciation for cultural dance and performance. In 1933, Dafora founded his production company, the African Opera and Dramatic Company, and dance company, Horton's Dancers. Kyonker or the Witch Woman was Dafora's most notable production. His work introduced American audiences to the humanity of native Africans.

4. **Bill "Bojangles" Robinson** (May 25, 1878–November 25, 1949) Bill "Bojangles" Robinson was a groundbreaking tap dancer since his childhood. He began performing at the age of twelve and became the first black solo act in vaudeville. Robinson transformed flat-footed hoofing style to performing

on his toes. His duet with Shirley Temple in film, The Little Colonel, made them the first on-screen interracial dancing couple. In 1989 a joint U.S. Senate/House resolution declared "National Tap Dance Day" to be May 25th, the anniversary of Robinson's birth.

5. **Carmen de Lavallade** (March 6, 1931) Carmen de Lavallade is a preeminent dancer and choreographer whose career spans over sixty years. De Lavallade went to high school with Alvin Ailey and invited him to his first ballet class, which sparked their long history of creating together and breaking barriers. Many ballets were created for her by Lester Horton, Alvin Ailey, Geoffrey Holder, Glen Tetley, John Butler, and Agnes de Mille. She made her Broadway debut in House of Flowers where she met her late husband, Geoffrey Holder. She also succeeded her cousin, Janet Collins, when she became a prima ballerina at the Metropolitan Opera. In 2012, de Lavallade received a Kennedy Center honor for her multifaceted career as an artist in dance, theater, film, television, and teaching.

6. **Debbie Allen** (January 16, 1950) Debbie Allen is a dancer, choreographer, director, singer, producer, activist, and actress. After being rejected by multiple institutions on racial grounds, she finally was secretly admitted into Houston Ballet School by a Russian dance instructor based on her superb talent. Post-graduating from Howard University, she took on Broadway and Hollywood. She starred in many Broadway shows including Sweet Charity, for which she received her first Tony award. Allen landed the role of the dance instructor in the dance movie "Fame." Allen made her directorial debut on "A Different World"- a spin-off of the Cosby Show that her sister Phylicia Rashad starred in. She opened her dance studio in 2011, Debbie Allen Dance Academy in Los Angeles, and continues to inspire many lives.

7. **Eartha Kitt** (January 17, 1927–December 25, 2008) Eartha Kitt was a dancer, singer, songwriter, comedian, actress, activist, and author. While studying at New York City's High School for Performing Arts, Eartha Kitt received a scholarship with the Katherine Dunham School of Dance and Theater. There she performed as a featured dancer and vocalist. Kitt made her Broadway debut in "Blue Holiday" and film debut in "Casbah." Her Broadway success in "New Faces of 1952' led to a recording contract with a succession of hit records including "Love for Sale," "I Want to Be Evil," "Santa Baby", and "Folk Tales of the Tribes of Africa." In 1967, she booked the role of "Catwoman" in the television series "Batman." Her signature purr during the series became world-renowned. She starred in films such as "St. Louis Blues" and "Anna Lucasta." Her final performance was for The HistoryMakers' an Evening with Eartha Kitt.

8. **Florence Mills** (January 25, 1896–November 1, 1927) Florence Mills was a dancer, choreographer, singer, actress, and comedian. She is credited as one of the leading performers of the Jazz Age. Mills was a pioneer for many blacks in theater and popularized syncopated dance and song. Mills and her sisters formed the vaudeville group, Mills Sisters, and performed around New York City. She booked her first lead role in the Broadway musical, Shuffle Along. Mill's commanding performance helped the show become an instant hit. She was known for her huge presence, high voice, and comedy. Mills starred in "From Dixie to Broadway," the first black Broadway musical with comedy. In 1926 she starred in "Blackbirds" where she sang "I'm a Little Blackbird Looking for a Bluebird. The song became her trademark and led to her being called Harlem's Blackbird.

9. **Frankie Manning** (May 26, 1914–April 27, 2009) Frankie Manning was a dancer, choreographer, and one of the founders of Lindy Hop. He revolutionized this style of dance in Harlem's legendary Savoy Ballroom with innovations such as the lindy air step and synchronized ensemble lindy routine. He won the 1989 Tony Award for his choreography in Black and Blue, and served as a consultant for and performed in Spike Lee's Malcolm X.

10. **Geoffrey Holder** (August 1, 1930–October 5, 2014) Geoffrey Holder was a dancer, choreographer, actor, director, singer, author, illustrator, and costume designer. His direction and costume design for the Broadway musical, The Wiz, won him a Tony Award in 1975. Along with theater work, Holder appeared in many films, notably the James Bond "Live and Let Die." He became a household name for his appearance in 7UP "Uncola" commercials.

11. **Janet Collins** (March 7, 1917–March 28, 2003) Janet Collins was a dancer, choreographer, and costume designer. She broke a major racial barrier when she became the Metropolitan Opera Ballet's first black prima ballerina. She performed in many vaudeville shows, Katherine Dunham's dance company, Broadway musicals, and as a soloist in her own productions. Her work Genesis was her last-known concert dance appearance.

12. **John W. Bubbles** (February 19, 1902–May 18, 1986)–John W. Bubbles was a tap dancer, choreographer, vaudevillian, pianist, and actor. He is known as the father of rhythm tap which consists of dropping heels on offbeat, using toes for accents, and extending rhythm patterns. He became the first black artist to appear on television after he performed in a duo "Buck and Bubbles" with pianist For Lee "Buck" Washington.

13. **Josephine Baker** (June 3, 1906-April 12, 1975) Josephine Baker was a dancer, singer, choreographer, actress, activist, WWII spy, and the world's first superstar. After dancing in many vaudeville shows, she joined the Broadway musical, Shuffle Along, which was the first successful all-black musical. She became well known after moving to France and performing her famous banana dance in La Revue Negre. Baker appeared in many films including The Sirens of the Tropics, Zou Zou, and Princesse TamTam. She released J'ai deux amours which became her most successful recording. Baker was one of the two women to speak at the March on Washington.

14. **Katherine Dunham** (June 22, 1909–May 21, 2006) Katherine Dunham was a dancer, choreographer, director, anthropologist, author, scholar, and founder of the Dunham Technique. After spending much time in the West Indies, Dunham returned and revolutionized American dance with folk & ethnic choreography. She opened two schools in Chicago where she taught over 150 black youth. She founded the Katherine Dunham Dance Company which propelled to receiving roles in television and film such as Cabin the Sky.

15. **Nicholas Brothers:** Fayard Nicholas (October 20, 1914–January 24, 2006); Harold Nicholas (March 2, 1921–July 3, 2000) The Nicholas Brothers were a tap-dancing duo whose creativity, excitement, innovative choreography, and fearlessness made them one of the greatest tap-dancing acts of all time. Brothers Fayard and Harold Nicholas combined jazz, ballet, and acrobatics to create what is known as "classical tap." After performing in many vaudeville shows, they appeared in over 30 Broadway musicals. Their acts consisted of acting, singing, and dancing so they were known as triple threats around the world. The best-known act was in the film Stormy Weather. The brothers danced around and through Cab Calloway and the orchestra with their famous split jumps down a flight of stairs.

16. **Norma Miller** (December 2, 1919–May 5, 2019) Norma Miller was a dancer, choreographer, author, comedian, and also known as the Queen of Swing. She is one of the creators of Lindy Hop and had a career that spanned over seven decades. While dancing at the Savoy Ballroom, she was discovered by legendary dancer Twist Mouth George at the vibrant age of twelve and had been in show business ever since. She has performed in many films such as A Day at the Races, Hellzapoppin, Stompin at the Savoy, and Malcolm X. Miller had a huge influence on the globalization of jazz culture and helped to preserve Lindy Hop.

17. **Pearl Primus** (November 29, 1919–October 29, 1994) Pearl Primus was a dancer, choreographer, and anthropologist. Her work focused on the African American experience and her research in Africa and in the Caribbean. Her first major work, African Ceremonial, reflected her early studies of her heritage. She formed her own company and was the director of the Performing Arts Centre in Liberia. Primus choreographed several pieces such as The Wedding for the Alvin Ailey American Dance Theater.

18. **Raven Wilkinson** (February 2, 1935–December 1, 2018) Raven Wilkinson was the first African American woman to dance full-time with the Ballet Russe de Monte Carlo. After being cut from the Ballet Russe audition twice, Wilkson remained undeterred. The former director, Frederic Franklin, pushed the company's leadership to look beyond her race. She became a soloist and danced many leading roles including the waltz solo in Les Sylphides. She joined Dutch National Ballet in Amsterdam where she felt much more accepted than in America. She later joined New York City Opera where she danced until she was 50 and continued there as an actress until 2011.

19. **Amber Barbee Pickens** (January 28, 1993) Amber Barbee Pickens is a dancer, choreographer, director, actress, author, illustrator, and designer. Raised in Dallas, Texas, Amber attended Booker T. Washington High School for the Performing and Visual Arts where she was honored by the Texas Commission on the Arts as a Young Master of the Arts. She also studied dance at Debbie Allen Dance Academy in Los Angeles and Alvin Ailey School in New York. At an early age, Amber was encouraged by her teachers to always give homage to the ones that paved the way. As a student at The Juilliard School, she sought more representation and spent many hours at the New York Public Library for Performing Arts learning more about legendary dancers such as Alvin Ailey, Eartha Kitt, the Nicholas Brothers and Josephine Baker. Amber was inspired and dedicated her career to uplifting and preserving the heritage of African Americans/ Blacks in the arts.

about amber

Amber Pickens is a graduate of The Juilliard School with a BFA in Dance. Raised in Dallas, Texas, at the early age of two, her mom enrolled her in ballet because she always was moving around. But while Amber favored acting and had big dreams of being a movie star, it was during the summer of her fourth-grade year when she attended The Debbie Allen Dance Academy Intensive at Texas Christian University that things shifted. That summer she fell in love and made her commitment to dance. Having realized that dance was not only a talent — but also her gift — it also brought much needed discipline and helped her better focus and realign her attitude. She saw how dance could open doors to many her many dreams i.e. Broadway, Film, Theater, and more.

With this newfound dedication to the arts, her appreciation for her craft blossomed even more. She became captivated with the history of ballet at W.E. Greiner middle school. Her dance teacher set pieces from Giselle and Swan Lake on the dance class, and Amber was fascinated. She then was accepted to the prestigious Booker T. Washington High School for the Performing and Visual Arts (HSPVA). There, Amber received the highest honor awarded to performing arts students in Texas. The Texas Commission of the Arts selected her as a Texas Young Master of the Arts, making her the first HSPVA freshman to be honored. She performed works by artists such as Robert Battle, Larry Keigwin, Dwight Rhoden, Kanji Segawa, Jessica Lang, Cherylyn Lavagnino, and Moussa Diabate. Throughout high school, Amber studied at the Dallas Theater Center, and played Moth in A Midsummer Night's Dream. Over the summers, Amber attended the American Black Film Festival, Camp Broadway, The Alvin Ailey School, Tasha Smith Acting Bootcamp, The Martha Graham School.

During her junior year at the HSPVA, she finally had the opportunity to see a live performance of Alvin Ailey American Dance Theater and realized she had never seen black people perform in the way that Ailey dancers did. She was amazed by the dancers' beauty and the many shades of brown uniting on stage. She learned more about the history of Ailey and wanted to be a part of this legacy.

During her time at The Juilliard School, Amber performed works by artists such as Pina Bausch, Camille Brown, Martha Graham, Lar Lubovitch, Jose Limon, Chase Brock, Murray Louis, Darrell Grand Moultrie, and Larry Keigwin. Amber is an advocate for community engagement in the arts and was part of the Juilliard PEPS (Performing Educational Programs for Schools), interactive dance performances for students in New York City middle and high schools.

Amber is a Dizzy Feet Foundation Award recipient. While attending Jacob's Pillow contemporary intensive, she received the Lorna Strassler Award for Student Excellence. Amber received an exciting opportunity to be a part of French Vogue's 14-page fashion photo shoot with infamous hip hop dancers, Les Twins photographed by Mario Sarrenti. You can also find her in Dior's New Looks table book. She graces eight pages in Redbook Magazine for new hot denim looks. She was titled as one of the top finalists for NBC Universal/ABFF's Star Project.

Amber gives ode to her grandmother's philosophy that "art belongs to the people, give back!" Paying homage to her grandmother who was a missionary in many communities, Pickens developed a nonprofit organization, Art Belongs to People (ABtP), that introduces the fundamentals of ballet and modern dance to children and youth during the summer. Her program exposes the art form to those who would not otherwise be privileged to the arts. Amber believes it is her responsibility as an ambassador of the arts to give back to her community and many others.

She started Art Belongs to People in May 2013 in Durban, South Africa teaching praise and modern dance for two weeks. She also taught modern dance at Kwa-Santi Secondary School for forty students ages 10-14 and praise dance to over a 100 church members ages 5-50 at Shalom church. From South Africa to the most underserved community in metro south Dallas, Pickens brought ABtP home to St. Philip's School and Community Center where she attended. ABtP is a reminder that everything she does in dance can be used as inspiration for children everywhere.

Amber made her Broadway debut in Cirque du Soleil's Paramour. She loves sharing the history and wisdom from professionals in entertainment, so Amber launched her talk show, Kickback & Chat with Amber Pickens. She was also featured as Grace Pressley on Law & Order SVU for their 21st season, making them the longest running TV series in New York City.

Amber Pickens definitely has a story to tell — her story — she sees dance an art form, its own language, a way of communicating. Even when surrounded with challenges, Amber stays focused on God's plan. "When a flower is blooming it doesn't look at the other flowers, it just blooms!"

Blooming in Motion is a love letter to all the black dancers that have paved and continue to pave the way for artists such as myself. The flowers throughout this book are symbols of gratitude towards the featured legends' sacrifice, perseverance, fearlessness, discipline, and eternal resilience. My mom introduced me to dance at the age of two when she enrolled me in ballet lessons. A few years later at ten, she signed me up for Debbie Allen's summer dance intensive where I learned about dancers from around the world. Ms. Allen encouraged me to honor and learn all styles of dance and use my gift to inspire others.

While studying at The Juilliard School, I experienced a tremendous time of doubt. I longed for representation and inclusion. Andra Corvino, my amazing ballet teacher, made sure I did not drop my crown, and introduced me to The Metropolitan's first black prima ballerina, the late Janet Collins. Seeing pictures of Ms. Collins reassured me that I belonged. I never knew that famous ballerinas could have curves! She fueled me to embrace every inch of myself-from my coarse curls to my hips! History serves as an eternal fire that continues to ignite me to my purpose. I am deeply rooted in the power of my ancestors. I want to continue uplifting black history and the importance of representation in the arts.

BLOOMING
IN
motion

CPSIA information can be obtained
at www.ICGtesting.com
Printed in the USA
LVHW071228190221
679365LV00005B/113